Holy Land Journal 2016

Carol Owen Reynolds

Holy Land Journal 2016
Carol Owen Reynolds
Published February 2026
Heirloom Editions
Imprint of Jan-Carol Publishing, Inc.

Graphic Design by Tara Sizemore

Cover photograph: Carol Owen Reynolds at Jacob's Well, the site of the encounter between the Samaritan woman and Jesus in John 4 of the Bible, where Jesus asks her for a drink of water. In the November 9th entry of Carol's journal, she describes how the famous "well" looks today.

ISBN: 978-1-970471-23-6
Library of Congress Control Number: On file

You may contact the publisher:
Jan-Carol Publishing, Inc.
PO Box 701
Johnson City, TN 37605
publisher@jancarolpublishing.com
www.jancarolpublishing.com

Also by Carol Owen Reynolds:

Fessenden! Looking Back on a Small-Town North Dakota Life

The Locas: A Collection of Stories about 13 "Crazy Women"

Stories from a North Dakota Cheerleader

LEBANON
UNDOF Zone
SYRIA
Qiryat Shemona
Golan Heights
Nahariyya
Akko
Sea of Galilee
Haifa
Tiberias
Nazareth
MEDITERRANEAN SEA
Jordan
Hadera
Janin
Netanya
Tulkarm
Nablus
Herzliyya
West Bank
Tel Aviv-Yafo
1994 Treaty Line
Bat Yam
AMMAN
Ramla
Ramallah
Rehovot
Jericho
Ashdod
JERUSALEM
Ashqelon
Bethlehem
Dead Sea
Qiryat Gat
Gaza
Hebron
Gaza Strip
1950 Armistice Line
Khan Yunis
Beersheba
1949 Armistice Line
ISRAEL
Dimona
Zefa
Zin
Negev
JORDAN
Mizpe Ramon
EGYPT
Sinai
Yotvata
Elat
40 km
40 mi
ADOBE STOCK

It seems like so very long ago, I began saving for a trip to the Holy Land so I could travel there *when I retired* (2006). I tucked away a small amount each payday for the trip of a lifetime. Then, just three months before retirement (March 2006), I met Chuck Reynolds, and all my plans for the rest of my life changed! Chuck was 16 years older than me but spry for his 81 years. We did go on a trip to Alaska, which was great—it was a cruise and had all the comforts of life.

Each time I mentioned the trip to the Holy Land, he would look at me like I had three heads, especially after his health began to fail a few years into the marriage. I think he believed he just could not keep up with the somewhat strenuous pace of a trip with a lot of walking and long plane trips. Even though I had enough saved for both of us, it just didn't happen. Then, Chuck died after 8 ½ years of marriage. My heart went out of rhythm, and I lost 35 pounds—so the trip was not to be, again.

July 2016, I got a clean bill of health from my doctor, and the same week, there was an announcement in the church bulletin of three trips to the Holy Land. I took it as a sign from God that the time had come for my long-awaited trip that I now call a "pilgrimage." I left emergency numbers with my family members, and I chose not to bring my cell phone or camera, determined to immerse myself fully in the experience.

Wednesday, November 2, 2016:

My friend, Pat Brooks, picked me up, and we had lunch at Cracker Barrel. Last night, I talked to my brothers, sister, Connie, Hella, Eddie, and some friends. I had supper with John and Samantha, and we talked about the upcoming presidential election. I had been the first person in Bristol, Va., to vote absentee (9/23/16) because I planned to be out of town on this "pilgrimage." I told my friend, Barry, that I had held my nose and voted for Trump because the bottom line, for me, is the stance I take on pro-life.

Barry said he voted early on October 31 and voted for Trump before lunch, because he was afraid if he voted after lunch, he might throw up! His reason for a Republican vote was that he wanted the Supreme Court stacked with conservative people, and presently, there is one vacancy with more vacancies expected in the near future considering the ages of the judges on the Court.

So, here I am, early, at the Tri-Cities Regional Airport. Shane had called this morning, and Connie called Pat's cell phone this afternoon. I elected to leave my cell phone at home. It is just one more thing to worry about. Besides, they all have my itinerary, and they can bring up pictures of my visitations and now are able to interpose my face, which they have seen too much of at times anyway!

In Atlanta, I will have to go to baggage claim and get my suitcase, then go back out and through security, then find my way to Turkish Air for my flight to Istanbul, where I will meet my group from Adriatic Pilgrimages.

I'm sitting here trying to figure out my pill-taking schedule to match the time difference. It seems the older I get, the more pills I take. There are several pain pills I take for my arthritis and for keeping my aged throat from closing. Then, there is the hormone pill to keep me from getting hot flashes, but the most critical pill is the one I take for incontinence! My son, John, says that is the pill he doesn't like to hear about, and generally, I give him too much information anyway.

Thursday, November 3, 2016 (12:05 pm):

If I could change something: It's too complicated to leave from Tri-Cities, because when you get to Atlanta, you have to go to baggage claim, then through that area, out to the exterior, and catch a shuttle to the International Terminal. Or I could have gotten better information from the tour company. I would have taken up the offer from my high school classmate, Dodie, and went to Georgia for a day and let her take me directly to the International Terminal to check in and go through security.

Turkish Air seemed very cordial and accommodating. The plane looked clean. I had to walk a long, long way to get to a central area, upstairs, in Istanbul. Then, *I misunderstood, thinking I should meet Adriatic here at Baggage Claim. Not so–I need to go on to Tel Aviv alone* again and then go through customs. It will be a long wait. I got my muffin and coffee. Don't forget: I need to take my incontinent pill! A man on the plane looked as if he had his pajamas on with a topcoat. May be a customary daily wear.

Many slept on the plane, some across unoccupied three-seat areas. I reclined and slept a couple hours. I rode with Marsha, a nice, friendly lady, originally from the Caribbean, who went to school in New York and stayed here. Married, divorced, son, and lives in Atlanta. She is an IT tech who works from home.

Small cup of coffee and a muffin: $9.00 plus a tip. Small price to pay so I can sit awhile. Too early to know which gate. Okay, so I'm too early to see the gate announcement and I thought I would meet my group by baggage claim, but NO! So, I did a lot of unnecessary walking. Where are they then? I wandered around and then found a seat near the food court. Nodded off a couple times. Finally, the gate announcement: #206. Another long walk.

I am questioned about my time in Israel. *I see my group!* I'm so happy! A whole passel of Philippine/Americans from California! I love these people! I worked with many of them for years. They are so caring and joyous. So far, I'm the only one with an old white head. It's just like the old days at Maternal and Child Health!

We arrive in Israel! We got through security and picked up our bags. We talked the whole time on the plane, in lines and on the bus, where we are waiting for them to find a lost bag. There is always one!

Friday, November 4, 2016:

Our guide, Johnny, still has youth and health on his side. He looks very much like the middle-aged Jewish men we will see now for a week, but he is Catholic, born and reared in Nazareth. Johnny has a slight accent and speaks several languages. As it will turn out, having a great guide will be the key to a successful pilgrimage.

The Grand Beach Hotel seems clean and comfortable, but I still can't sleep because I'm so excited. I only get about two hours of rest. My Filipino friends are very conscious of my care and safety. They are always watching to make sure I'm okay.

Johnny is telling us the story of the Cedar Tree and Simon the Tanner. Also, of King Solomon, the first builder of the Temple Mount. Fr. Melanio served Mass at St. Peter's in Jaffa, across from Tel Aviv. I prayed for Eileen, who I promised I would pray for just before her death. The church faces the sea and is run by the Franciscan Friars. He reminded us that we are first the citizens of the Kingdom of God. Adjoining the Church is the house of Simon the Tanner, where St. Peter heard the message, "Kill and eat."

Our bus is passing by the Mediterranean Sea today, and there is lots of traffic. We see the various embassies, including the U.S. Embassy. Tel Aviv is the largest city, then Jerusalem, then Haifa, the most beautiful, where "they go to pamper themselves." (*After my return, there is arson here and arrests are made for terrorism.*) Israel has lots of rich soil and water. That is why it is called the "Land of Milk and Honey." We saw Mt. Carmel, where we visit the Carmelite Monastery and Church of El Muhraka, where Elijah challenged the priests of Baal.

Because Johnny is from Nazareth, he has a rich knowledge of the city. He especially knows about the Church of the Annunciation, because it is his parish and he went to school there for 12 years. He also got married and baptized his children in his parish church. He showed us some of the layers of the ground that have been built after different destructions of the city. We can literally see where Jesus walked. The city was very small, therefore the old question, "What good could come out of Nazareth?" Of course, Johnny said that two good things came out of Nazareth: Jesus, our Lord, and Johnny! Only

32 families still survive in the city that can be traced back to the time of Christ, and Johnny is from one of these families.

We went to Mary's Well, where some say the Annunciation occurred. However, he says she was frightened away and only heard the first two words: "Hail Mary." She ran home and heard the remainder of the message from the Archangel.

A couple more ladies have joined our group today, one from the East Coast. The picture taking is crazy. Everyone is taking pictures of everything and everyone else, selfies and all. It is too much.

My feet and ankles are swollen, and I'm very tired but need to go down for supper, then to bed. I must get up at 5:30am, be down for breakfast by 6:30am, and out of here by 7:30am. It will be a long day tomorrow. The couples are going to have their marriages blessed at Cana, so the wives were asked to bring white dresses. I wish Chuck was here for this. He never would have made it with all the walking.

Saturday, November 5, 2016:

Again, I got little sleep, and I had chest pain in the morning. My feet and ankles are still swollen. We will stay here at the Golden Crown Hotel for two nights. I'm tired before we even get started! Ladies in their white look lovely and are glowing. Their husbands are proud and like the attention (obviously)!

We pray, and we will celebrate Mass every day. Today, we will celebrate at Cana, where Jesus performed his first miracle, changing water into wine. Cana is a direct opposite in relation to Haifa in cleanliness. Too many people to keep the streets clean. Trash stacked everywhere and souvenirs are hanging, lying, stacked, and being carried everywhere. There are huge tourist buses with expert drivers pulling in and out just inches from one another; thousands of tourists and locals are dodging in and out.

Our priest, Fr. Melanio; tour host, Tessie; and Johnny do a great job of keeping us together. There is always a straggler to wait for on the bus and at each site. Kathleen seems, and admits to, having tremors. She asks a lot of questions. So, the group makes it to the church and a nun greets us for our reservation to watch nine couples renew their wedding vows during Mass. The church is quite clean—anyway, as clean as can be expected in this organized chaos!

In my mind, I'm renewing my vows to Chuck. I know his spirit hangs by me. It is bittersweet. There is a lot of noise from other groups coming in, and I try to help the host get their attention from a wrought iron opening on the side and shush them, but it is almost impossible.

The little ceremony goes off to the pleasure and acceptance of the couples. Mass is over; congratulations all around, and we are herded off to the wine shop for a toast and to check out the souvenirs. We get a little, and I mean little, glass of wine. Kathleen spills her wine down the front of me and it hits my scarf, T-shirt, badge holder, and shoes (white tennis shoes). How could such a small amount of wine cover so much territory? She apologizes twice, profusely, and we go on. Here in this mess of humanity, I must be pulling up all the forgiveness I can muster from Dear God.

Before I left home, I knew the boat ride on the Sea of Galilee would be a highlight, and it was! I'm crying when they raise the American flag and the Philippine flag, and we sing our National Anthem. Again, we pray and hear scripture, tying us to the place. We are taught to dance like the Jewish people; there is line dancing and rock and roll! How beautiful is this place, where cold air and warm air rise above the water where Jesus walked! A kibbutz still exists here that was set up to build the grounds and make a place for the tourists.

And to think how easy it would have been to just turn over this morning and tell my group to go on and enjoy the day! I did not actually touch the water here. Later, we took a ride stop, not on our schedule, at the First House of Peter where Jesus waited for the Apostles to bring him fish to restore their bodies and souls. Here, I touched the water and blessed myself with it as it slowly lapped over the rocky shore.

At Capernaum, we truly walked where Jesus walked, preached, and lived with the Apostles. In all these places, we can see layers of destruction from different occupations. They found the house of Jesus and Peter when they found the rock inside it. The church and many areas are built in octangular shapes.

I'm walking slowly. I am tired. My irregular heartbeat seems better here, probably from the dry air. So often, I would like to be alone, but my friends keep me in their sight at all times. I keep falling asleep on the bus (sitting up) and I decide not to try the last visit of the day at the Mount of Beatitudes. It's okay. I know I was here.

We stop at a place where they sell a lot of anointing oil and food. Certainly a few souvenirs. I was able to get a couple bananas for my tired leg cramps. A banana, an energy bar, and some raisins are my supper in my room. I wasn't very hungry anyway after a very good piece of chicken for lunch. I didn't want to put on my happy face, because I was anxious to wash off the wine from the Cana spillover! My T-shirt ended up in the trash because the stains had taken over.

I watch a little CNN and Fox News, the only English-speaking channels, to see that the race for President of the United States is neck and neck! They are saying we may not know the results on Tuesday, November 8th, or even later than that, because of election fraud and hacking into voter websites. I slept like a rock from 7pm to 11pm. Now, at 1:30am, I'm awake, writing and checking out my swollen ankles and broken leg veins!

Sunday, November 6, 2016:

So much driving today, but not as tired, because I slept more hours. Today, the Christians worship, but other religions have a regular workday. If your employer is not of your religion, then you are allowed to work at his place of employment.

We are told we are to have our passports ready when we go into the Palestinian Authority. Also, that as we cross over into their area, we do not take pictures at their border.

We cannot ride our big bus up the winding, steep climb of Mt. Tabor, the place of the Transfiguration, so we ride in the smaller buses that hold only about 10 people. I saw a couple crosses with the Lord's Prayer on them. They have some of the soil from Mt. Tabor on them, and I'm thinking they would make great Christmas gifts for my grandchildren.

The view from the top is spectacular! The fields below are blocked off in many colors, reflecting the crops grown in the lush valleys. Here is the church where Mass is being said below the giant dome. Our Mass is later at Shepherd's Field. So many people, so many cameras. Many caught up in the beauty of today. Others more caught up in the camera taking and chatting about their photography skills. It occurs to me that someday in the future, easy access to these places may not be allowed, in order to preserve their magnificence.

We have lunch at Jericho, the oldest city in the world. I have never seen poverty as I see it here. Many street people selling souvenirs, even a boy trying to sell a pack of Wrigley's Spearmint gum. We hold tight to our handbags. The lunch was okay, but I didn't eat too much of it with my conscience creeping up on me for being so blessed with so much on the other side of the world.

The River Jordan is not as clean and as wide as I expected it to be, in comparison to the Sea of Galilee. The atmosphere is teeming with excitement as some are being baptized by full immersion. We, however, just hold our heads down, and Fr. Melanio dips water over our heads. I was originally baptized 56 years ago, at age 19, in an El Cajon, California, church called Our Lady of Grace. The contrast is too much to think about today.

Bedouins in the desert live like I had imagined them existing: just living in dirt, scratching out life from sand and stricken animals. Here, again, the feelings of my many gifts tug at my conscience. We celebrate Mass at Shepherd's Field. A cool wind has come up and I shiver in the shade. Then, the walk back to the bus.

When we pass into Bethlehem, we do see border guards, but there is peaceful and cordial existence. There seems to be respect here; in other words, "You treat us with respect, and we will treat you with respect."

We must hurry to get to the Church of the Nativity, the oldest church in the world, before they close at 5pm. Thanks to Johnny's influence with the police and Greek Orthodox leaders, we get in and stand in line a long time. He gives us a history lesson and our instructions on how to behave here, i.e. remember to sit in the altar area with legs uncrossed, as it is a sign of rudeness and disrespect in their culture to cross our legs. Five or six of us are taken farther up the line to kiss the place where our Lord was born. This will, no doubt, be a once-in-a-lifetime experience.

In order to survive in Bethlehem, a small group is doing business and is in the West Bank of Christians, who depend on the tourist trade because of an original business license. They are honest and friends of our Johnny, so it is the place to get authentic gold and cedar wood products produced *here* in Bethlehem, and they stay open late on Sunday just for us.

I go a little shopping crazy here, and then I'm embarrassed because my new Visa card is "declined" at first, probably because I had not told the credit union I would be using it on the West Bank. I am ready to give up when one of the managers takes me in the office with him to make a call that saves my shopping spree. He made the life-saving call that provided me with an explanation later, over the bus microphone, saying the reason they wanted me in the office was so they could tell me to, "Put my hands behind my back!" It is amusing to me that a couple women want to know the grand total of my shopping excursion, and I can only say that it was, "A LOT!"

Here we are at the Grand Court in Jerusalem. Beautiful and clean. I even have a glass of wine with dinner, the first time in years. Life is good.

Monday, November 7, 2016:

I only slept about three hours total (in spots) as my mind was racing. I'm tired but trust in God to get me through the day. Because my father was a Welshman, I stood by the Welsh "Our Father" at the Church of Pater Noster. Here, the Our Father is inscribed on the walls of the church in 140 languages.

We visit churches at the Mount of Olives. Beautiful. Lots of prayers for our loved ones, and we stand in long lines, and there are so many people and so much picture taking. I'm becoming acquainted with my new friends.

Old, old trees in the Garden of Gethsemane. Where did Jesus sit? Under which tree? Had He, at one time, sat under all the trees? Some trees are from before the time of Christ and others are new. Some trees are even planted by popes in recent history.

Jerusalem! Fantastic! Beyond all expectations! We hear its history and soak up its beauty as Johnny tells us its details. He is so well versed in everything in the Holy Land, and he knows how to teach and control our group. What an expansive mind! He speaks many languages and has contact with all the local people who can get us the best spots and advantages so we don't miss anything. We are standing across from the Eastern Wall that some say is the point where Christ will return. Even though it is cemented shut, I doubt that will be a problem for Our Lord, if in fact, he does return to that place.

ADOBE STOCK

Johnny, Tess (the host), and Fr. Melanio are always counting to be sure we don't lose anyone in this crush of humanity. I do the reading at the Mass today that is held on the Palestinian Authority. It's true that there is respect among the many different people here. I do think that they need each other, so that helps them co-exist peacefully.

Chicken is mostly my food of choice. I'm not interested in lamb or a lot of vegetables, and I drink bottled water only.

We visit the Dead Sea. It is smaller now for lack of a fresh water source. Someday it will be gone completely. When? I ask Tess. Maybe then, God will return. People are industrious and make expensive products for beauty and health from the beach minerals.

I had passed out slightly a bit earlier, and my coach mate, who has been an ICU nurse for 41 years, was saying, "My friend, my friend, are you fainting?" I said I was okay, just tired. So tired.

I take a nap for 20 minutes at the water's edge while the others go in the water. Some immerse as much as possible, some only wading, and my friend Virginia (from Las Vegas) fell face first in the sandy, salty water! She kept her eyes closed until after they led her to the shower! Poor thing! She handled it so well. She is an experienced traveler and things are taken as they come. Virginia is vivacious, in good shape, and is a proud single mother of two boys who have both been very successful.

I like everything about Virginia, except her eating habits, and I tell her so—she has to try a taste of everything but takes large portions and wastes too much. I am open with her about my feelings, and I trust her to hold my history to herself.

Everyone is tired and will go to bed early, because Johnny says that tomorrow is the highlight of our pilgrimage. Fox News is the only English-speaking news here, and they say the e-mail scandal is over and unchanged. I think the majority of our group is liberal.

Tuesday, November 8, 2016:
(Election Day in the USA)

We started so early: 6:30am! Johnny knows where everything is in the Holy Land! Our group sees more churches, tombs, shopping areas, and where to eat than anyone in the place! We see *so much* more than most.

Lots and lots of walking! (Johnny warned us.) Via Dolorosa: I get to carry the cross that is lightweight, not like the heavy cross Jesus carried, and I share it with three others. We pause at each station for the readings. Here, on this very street, is where Jesus carried the cross so long ago, and I now have the privilege of walking in His actual footsteps. We see where Jesus died; where he was anointed and where he was buried in the tomb. There is no way I can describe the impact this place had on me. I removed my shoes, kept them, and never wore them again. We had the best food ever at Notre Dame Cafeteria. The very best food so far!

Shoes I wore while walking in the footsteps of Christ. I've never worn them since.

I didn't know that men and women were separated at the Wailing Wall. Here, I prayed for the conversion of people who have been a part of my family for the last couple of years and for return to the faith of people in my family who have fallen away. I also did not know that when we are through praying at the Wall, we had to back away—not turn and walk away from it. Interesting.

Mary's home. Mary's place, where she was taken up to Heaven! I saw things today I never saw before and will never see again. Unbelievable beauty and cleanliness, and unbelievable poverty and hopelessness (because of the lack of leadership in Palestine). There are places where men must be at the locations each day to maintain authority or hand over the keys and lose the location.

Johnny is even smarter than I ever thought. In addition to speaking several languages, he has a great education that included some teaching in Rome. He has the gift of teaching. I can compare him, now, as I see other groups coming through the sites.

My friend, Virginia, spends money every time she turns around, and she buys expensive things. I have discovered she has another bad habit of showing what she has in her wallet around people who truly do not need to see it. She is wrong to do this, and she happily accepts my appraisal of her conduct.

Virginia and Tessie take my picture several times at the Church of St. Anne, the grandmother of Jesus and mother of Mary. We also saw the Church of Martha, and Lazarus, run by the Friars, who work so hard to keep the church going and safe. This day was truly the highlight Johnny promised us.

I wish you could see the buses and bus drivers. Huge buses coming within inches of each other. These drivers are so fabulous and good at what they do. I was glad I slept so well last night. I only missed one thing (Peter's Tomb) because I had to sit and rest, and the bunion on my left foot was hurting. We had a 12-hour day, and I wonder what tomorrow will bring. I'm sure it can't be better than today.

Wednesday, November 9, 2016:
(Donald Trump will be the President-Elect)

Another day of a full schedule of seeing churches, shopping, and eating. I am learning to eat and sleep better. At the Church of St. Elizabeth, we hear about Mary's visit to her and the story about Zechariah becoming mute. I kept looking for something of St. John the Baptist and they had only two olivewood statues left, so I can give a gift of St. John the Baptist to John Criswell, as it is his patron saint.

Earlier, we had Mass at Our Lady of the Ark, where I found cashmere scarves for a good price that will make wonderful Christmas gifts. We saw the Parliament buildings off in the distance. Jewish people pay almost 50% of their income to taxes, so the streets, utilities, buses, and bullet trains all work perfectly.

The opposite is quite true in Samaria where life is from hand to mouth. There, little boys are selling soap bars, and some of the buildings are so dirty, it looks like they smeared black grease on the sides. There are hulls and car parts stacked up on the streets. I wonder if the only secure jobs are those of being police or military people in these parts of a land that, in spite of its hopelessness, is a place where they can survive and live a somewhat decent life.

We see, at Jacob's Well, that it has only become a tourist trap. This is a sad end of a beautiful story of our Lord and the Samaritan woman. The water is drinkable, even today, and it is a deep, deep well! There is a cleric here who has painted hundreds of great icons and sells them right near the well. He spoke several languages. His story is that he has prepared for his resting place, a crypt that he has designed and sits by the front of the church—now a tourist trap with beautiful artwork. Only about six or seven Christians live here, so they probably live a very quiet life!

Johnny and Mohammed (the bus driver) leave us tomorrow as we proceed to the border crossing of Jordan. We have a little gathering of thankfulness for their service to us, and they are given gifts of money and cards of thanks. We have a small toast to them and to Tessie Lightholder, our host. Then, Fr. Melanio blesses all our souvenirs, jewelry, etc.

Everything must be ready in our suitcases to be set out at 5:30am! We are to be downstairs by 6am so they can load up the luggage, and we can be out of here by 7am after breakfast. Tough schedule. Virginia leaves us tomorrow, also, on her way to the diamond exchange and to her many travels. It will be hard to say goodbye to my new friend.

Hillary Clinton and Donald Trump have made conciliatory statements. There are protest marches in some of the large cities in the United States.

Thursday, November 10, 2016:

Virginia is leaving this morning, and I give her many compliments. Then, at the table, I told everyone that I would tell them how I really feel about her when she is gone! When we dropped her off, after a lot of hugs and good wishes, Fr. Melanio asked, in the presence of all, “Carol, tell us now how you really feel.” I said, “She doesn’t know how to eat!” This is true because she wastes food. She may take a big bite from a slice of bread, from the center, and throw away the rest!

She also pushes her half-eaten food to the center of the table. I say that she lives "large."

Goodbye, Jerusalem. Last looks of the city of our God, the places He lived and walked. Now, I have some of the soil on my shoes. We stop briefly in Jericho, the City of Perfumes and the oldest city in the world. About 25,000 Muslims occupy the city, and there are only about 500 Christians. This is the place of the Sycamore tree where the man of small stature climbed up to see Jesus. There is a monastery at the side of a hill, built in 1906. Jesus wandered in this wilderness for 40 days. He was tempted by the Devil. He didn't eat for 40 days.

We see herds of sheep and goats. The shepherds ride on donkeys or walk. Jesus said, "I know my sheep and my sheep know me." Another truth. We see camels, too, which are still used for transportation today.

About 9:30am, we enter Jordan. We go through a checkpoint and show our passports. We wave goodbye to Johnny and Mohammed. The customs people take our passports and manifest, and we wait. Our new guide is Ruby. We are fortunate, they say, that we have a tourist police with us. We see King Hussein Bridge.

This is the kingdom of Moses. We go to St. George Church. There is a mosaic on the floor that has been uncovered from centuries ago. We also have lunch in Madaba. Mt. Nebo is Moses's mountain. He died at age 120. The church sits atop Mt. Nebo and was originally built in AD 93. It has just been renovated by building over the top of the original church, leaving walkways open to see the original church and mosaic floors. Some pieces of the old columns line the center.

We celebrate Mass and, on the way back, visit a mosaic shop. Here, they also create the mosaics (very expensive) that can be delivered to your home by DHL. Families here build second stories on their homes for children who can bring their spouses to live upstairs. Ordinarily, the daughters and daughters-in-law take advantage of the mothers and mothers-in-law who can cook! This way, families can stay together and fight together!

This is how they build their houses—with the upper floors prepared for their sons to live above their parents. I can't help but think, "The brides had better get along with their mothers-in-law!"

We will be going to Petra tomorrow, and they are saying it is a long walk or a small carriage ride into the canyon road. I have no idea what to expect, as I know nothing about Petra.

Friday, November 11, 2016:

Petra (Peter) is the place of the Nabataean Empire that existed between 400 B.C. and AD 106. The city and tombs are carved out of the stones of the canyon. It was empty until the 1800s when it was discovered. Some of the scenes from *Indiana Jones and the Last Crusade* were filmed in Petra.

Some people believe that Petra is the place where Moses struck his staff and brought forth water. Some people believe that when Christ returns, it will be to Petra.

Petra is about four hours away from the Ramada, where we are staying. I'm having digestive problems, but I'm able to go on with everyone and keep my troubles to myself.

We get a late start because we can't find one of the ladies. Filippino people tend to raise their voice, especially when they get excited or nervous, so the pitch is getting higher and higher. For 15 minutes, Tessie and another person go back in the hotel to search while we wait in the bus. 15 minutes later, we find our missing lady sitting quietly in the back of the bus praying the rosary!

When things happen out of the ordinary, my group looks at me to see my reaction. This time, I just shake my head and laugh. A difference in praying the rosary for them is that the leader prays every other decade in reverse (i.e. first decade, leader: *Holy Mary, full of grace*; second decade, leader: *Holy Mary, Mother of God*). Also, I don't know several of the songs at Mass (which is every day) that they have memorized.

Ruby gives us a history of the Jordan royal family during our ride. I have always been fascinated with King Abdullah, who didn't want the job. In my work experience, it is said to always pick the person who doesn't want the job, because that is the one who understands what is involved in the work. There are pictures of the King and some of his family everywhere. He is loved in his country.

A short stop at the W.C. (water closet). At first, I thought it meant "Women and Children." I got coins for Shane Michael at this stop. We also get the best bananas in the world in Jordan.

I keep mulling over in my mind what I'm going to do. Should I walk or take the carriage ride? It is $20 with tip each way. Money is not the problem. It's a question of whether or not I can make the walk. Or, can I make the walk one way? Tessie thinks I can make the walk and encourages me. Near the beginning, an older lady, about 60, warns me not to try it. She says she had to stop halfway and didn't see the best part.

We start down the canyon, and we are swarmed with young boys selling cheap silver bracelets, who think nothing of "getting in our space." I hold my hand over the money in my pocket. At one point, I get dizzy from having a boy get just a couple inches from my face. Tessie does a remarkable job of keeping them away in comparison to other guides.

The columns of the canyon remind me of Zion National Park, but on steroids. Tessie keeps encouraging me to continue when I ask, "How much farther?" She keeps telling me it's going to be worth it in the end. And it is! It is not called "One of the New Seven Wonders" for nothing. Not only does the carving of the Treasury amaze me, but also the conglomeration of life in the circle of tombs. Camels with bright colored blankets on their backs are set in a circle, waiting for passengers at $5.00 a ride.

Some of the group ride the camels and take pictures. They look somewhat like Jordan citizens with the scarves they bought at the gift shops on the way down. The bunion on my foot is beginning to hurt, and I'm very tired. I tell Tessie I will elect to take a carriage ride along with another lady back up the canyon.

This picture was taken at Petra in Jordan.

This carriage ride is definitely not for sissies! My partner haggles with the driver over the price and it turns out they were each defending the same thing! The carriage bounces a couple feet off the rocky surface, and I hold on tight to the loops above my head. Mom would have been proud of me, and I can see her right there with me. She liked impulsive things like this ride.

The horses are so strong but seem thin to me. I can't help but think what their life is like: up and down the canyon every day, hauling at least three people each time in the tiny carriage. Poor horses. Really? Would they have a chance to live at all if it wasn't for these carriage rides? I doubt it.

A few of us gather at the start of the walk, and while we wait, my carriage partner, Zita, tells corny jokes. We roar with laughter as if it's the funniest thing we ever heard. It's comic relief.

I had lentil soup, pita bread, and dessert for lunch. Then we hit the road. I have made the mistake of sitting near the back of the bus without shock absorbers. Pain. Pain in the neck, pain in the back, pain in the bunion in my foot. We're bouncing all over the bumpy road. I think it's my problem *only* because everyone else seems to have conked out and are enjoying a beautiful nap.

It gets dark early and I endure the ride until we get to Ruby's parish church for Mass, Church of Martyrs. It is difficult to concentrate on the Mass, but again, I endure. Then, we continue on to the Ramada for supper before we even go up to our rooms. I tell Tessie to cancel my wake-up call and that I am willing to pay for my box lunch I have ordered for tomorrow, but that I just can't leave the hotel.

Tessie, who always takes care of everyone, understands. I think I shall owe some money for tips she collects in one big fund for the driver and Ruby. There are probably others she tips to keep the politics going that she conducts as part of her job. She always tries to get the very best for her people and always thinks of us first. She is gracious, and she is a hugger!

I take a shower, watch television briefly, and sleep for 12 hours. I am weak, and I am awestruck from what I have seen. I'm so glad I came to Petra. There were times I thought it might not be a good idea.

Saturday, November 12, 2016:

(in the hotel)

I spent all day at the hotel. I slept a lot and ate lunch at the hotel restaurant. I checked the price of a carved metal set of a family of chickens, thinking it would be inexpensive and fit nicely in my kitchen. WRONG! $180 but could get it at a bargain price for $140. I have also considered getting a traditional garment, but the price is about $500, and I couldn't see when and where I would use it, other than to give a talk about my pilgrimage.

I had supper with the group and a thank-you session. They will pick up our luggage at 1:30am by the room door. Bus leaves at 3am for the airport.

Sunday, November 13, 2016:

Up at 1am, and we left at 3am for the airport. At the Amman Airport, I thought I was in the wrong bathroom because the only place to go was a hole in the floor! Oh well! I guess we should all try lots of new experiences, even this late in life.

I got a Starbucks coffee, and it cost nearly $10 in US money. I was assured I could use the Jordan money I got in change when I got to Istanbul. WRONG AGAIN!

I just can't quite understand the burqa. I'm not sure I'll ever make sense of it, even though I know it's an important part of their religion and culture.

So, I got a Turkish ice cream. It is sticky, almost like gum. Totally tasteless. My group leaves me alone about noon at the airport in Istanbul. It's a sad day. We have had a terrific time together. Hopefully, we will see each other again.

No one will give me a seat; not even a man will give this old lady a place on the central waiting area. There is an unoccupied seat next to a young woman, and I ask to sit down. She points to her friend, who she is saving the seat for and who is on her cell phone. No seat for me.

Finally, *finally* my flight gate is posted and I get on a plane to go home. There is a 12-hour flight ahead and about 300 people on the plane, and I am very tired but can't sleep. I am up and down all the way to Atlanta. I do get to watch the fourth quarter of the Eagles game and see my favorite North Dakota quarterback, Carson Wentz.

When I go through customs in Atlanta, I must have looked like the wrath of God. The customs agent chuckled and asked which countries I had visited. I named them off. He asked if I bought anything, and I said I had gotten a lot of sh**t I didn't need. He laughed and said, "Get out of here!"

The rat race begins in Atlanta, and thanks to a sharp, speedy young man, I make it to the plane headed for the Tri-Cities. I am the last to board the plane. I remember the plane taking off, but I don't remember the last leg of the trip because I have passed out from exhaustion.

Things I Would Do the Same:

- Room alone
- Take lots of snacks
- Leave my camera at home
- Identify my town by the GEICO commercial of the gecko performing on State Street (Bristol, TN/VA)

Things I Would Do Different:

- Leave from Atlanta
- Wear compression socks
- Try to take more notes during the day when we are on the bus
- Wear lightweight clothing
- Bring more money *or* another credit card *or* raise the limit on the card I take

To use an old cliché: It truly was the trip of a lifetime!

Questions?

About the Author

Always writing, Carol Owen Reynolds authors short stories just like many of you play golf, go fishing, or make crafts for your homes. The short stories that preceded her first book, *Stories from a North Dakota Cheerleader*, earned her a letter of congratulations from Governor Doug Burgum after she took a chance and sent him a copy.

Carol's skill at putting thoughts into words was encouraged early on by her high school teacher, Elizabeth Pfeiffer. Later in life, Carol sought creative writing classes at Grossmont College in El Cajon, California.

Her second book, *The Locas: A Collection of Stories about 13 "Crazy Women"*, explores Carol's life before and after a spiritual awakening influenced by a Catholic Cursillo retreat (known in the Protestant faith as the Walk to Emmaus). *Fessenden! Looking Back on a Small-Town North Dakota Life* reflected on the community that shaped her, while *Holy Land Journal 2016*, her fourth published book, chronicles her spiritual journey through one of the world's most sacred landscapes.

Words of encouragement are welcome and may be sent to Jan-Carol Publishing at communications@jancarolpublishing.com.

www.ingramcontent.com/pod-product-compliance
Lightning Source LLC
LaVergne TN
LVHW021628120826
845149LV00023B/1491

9781970471236